# Down & Dirty
## to 180⁰

# Down & Dirty
# to 180⁰

*A Mother's Memoir of Her*
*Daughter's Domestic Violence*

Margaret M. Hodges

# Dedication

**This book is dedicated to my family**

### TO MY HUSBAND

Thank you for your understanding and support. In many ways, you gave encouragement without realizing it, and that love is invaluable.

### TO MY DAUGHTER and SON

God blessed me with you. I am blessed our lives have been enriched with love and watching you grow to become independent Christ-loving adults. Continue to keep Christ first in your lives. His and my love are unconditional and never-ending.

### TO MY GRANDCHILDREN

You make life fun and exciting. It is a blessing from God to have you in my life. Keep God first and, as you grow older, God will always be with you.

### TO MY BROTHERS

May God always touch you, as you serve and touch others. Continue to keep God with you.

# Acknowledgments

First and foremost, I would like to thank God for loving my family and me and giving us the strength to endure, learn and educate others.

Thanks to Dr. David Banks for helping me find my purpose.

Thanks to Serious Writers' Accountability and Training (S.W.A.T.) Book Camp and Coach Laura Brown for your guidance.

Thanks to my mentors Dr. Sharon Cannon and Vincent I. Phipps for encouraging me to see the future through communication.

Thanks to Andrea Hodges for the cover design.

Thanks to Reginald Hodges for the cover art.

Thanks to Tamika Johnson for encouraging me to birth a book.

Thank you, Felice Smith Lowe, for the strength and encouragement you have always given me.

Thanks to editor Maria Noel and the beta readers, Ruth Ann Bard, Carolyn Boyd, Reverend Harry Cooper Jr., Esterrell Evans, Vanessa G. Hodges, PhD., Marcia McGraw, Jacqueline Strong-Moss, Esq. Words cannot express my gratitude for your advice.

Thanks to the Reading Between the Wines book club for bringing books back into my life.

The Dream Team

# Table of Contents

INTRODUCTION ............................................................................... 13

CHAPTER 1 LIFE GOT REAL......................................................... 15

ONCE UPON A TIME ............................................................................. 16

MISSED SIGNS ..................................................................................... 21

THE ESTEEMED HIGH SCHOOL............................................................. 24

MS. INDEPENDENCE, ON THE ROAD TO COLLEGE ................................ 26

RING, RING ......................................................................................... 29

AND THE DOORBELL RANG .................................................................. 31

PLANTING THE SEED ............................................................................ 33

WHAT'S A MOTHER TO DO? ................................................................ 35

YOU PULLED THE TRIGGER................................................................... 38

NOT PICTURE PERFECT......................................................................... 41

NOTES FROM MOM ............................................................................. 43

CHAPTER 2   LEARNING SURVIVAL TECHNIQUES ......................... 45

DOWN & D.I.R.T.Y. TO 180° TECHNIQUE ............................................ 46

DISCIPLINE YOURSELF........................................................................... 46

IMAGINE THE OUTCOME ...................................................................... 48

REALIZING THE RETURN ON YOUR INVESTMENT.................................... 50

TACTIC IMPLEMENTATION .................................................................... 52

YOU FOR YOU ..................................................................................... 56

CHAPTER 3   THE POWER OF  PERSUASION................................. 61

THE CYCLE OF DOMESTIC VIOLENCE..................................................... 62

POWER AND CONTROL WHEEL ............................................................. 64

JANELLE'S STORIES............................................................................... 65

NOTES FROM MOM ............................................................................. 82

MASTER MANIPULATORS - WHAT ABUSERS SAY? .................................. 83

**CHAPTER 4  GETTING READY** ....................................................................... 87

    START NOW AND PREPARE ............................................................... 88

    AN EXAMPLE OF HOMETOWN SERVICES ............................................... 91

    EXIT PREPAREDNESS ...................................................................... 94

    7 STAGES OF GRIEF ...................................................................... 97

**CHAPTER 5  JANELLE'S REFLECTIONS** ....................................................... 101

    JANELLE ON THE 7 STAGES OF GRIEF ................................................. 102

    MESSAGES FROM JANELLE SHARED OVER THE INTERNET ....................... 104

    LETTER TO JANELLE ..................................................................... 107

    NOTES FROM MOM ...................................................................... 110

**RESOURCES** .............................................................................................. 113

**ABOUT THE AUTHOR** .............................................................................. 119

# Introduction

This book is written for parents, family, friends, loved ones, and those experiencing domestic violence. I hope the information is useful and can be applied to make a better life for you, your family or someone you know.

People can be cruel and treat you like dirt, something to be walked on, treated poorly, and not cared about. If this is you, know that life can possibly turn around 180°.

Caring for yourself is like adding beneficial nutrients to the soil. With proper care, growth happens. People have come away from domestic violence to lead loving and productive lives.

Down & Dirty to 180° has practical principles to help overcome Domestic Violence and become a Survivor. Janelle, the daughter, in the following pages is one such person.

Janelle's marriage began in 2008 and ended in 2012. The following stories are placed randomly and may seem out of order. Recalling each of the stories seems like yesterday.

# Chapter 1

# Life Got Real

*"Every flower must grow through dirt."*
**Laurie Jean Sennott**

# Once Upon a Time

Once upon a time… isn't that how fairytales begin? That's how I thought my life would be, living in a fairytale. I lived with both my parents under the same roof growing up. I finished Northview High School in Manchester, Georgia, just outside of Atlanta. I graduated high school at 16 and went to college. At first, I was going to attend the Fashion Institute of Technology (F.I.T.) in New York but decided against it. At 16 I thought I was mature enough to handle life. I thought I was grown. I finished high school with a scholarship. I accepted the letter into the college of my choice. I chose a college out of state because I was afraid of getting trapped in the Atlanta life and not being able to handle it.

After graduation and before college, I dated, partied, and worked. I went on a date, and my date paid for the dinner and movie. When my date walked me home, we kissed goodnight on my front porch. I thought that was it. He wanted me to "go down" on him. That wasn't my thing, oral sex. He hauled off and slapped me. It stunned me, and I kicked him and said, "Put your hands on me again, and I'll get one of my father's guns and shoot the crap out of you, now get out of here." I don't know if I would have shot him or not, but I would not stand for someone putting their hands on me.

I realized there are different layers I should do in life, different orders or steps to the way things should be done. Moving fast and needing to slow down, my slow down came in the form of Bennett College in Greensboro, North Carolina. Bennett College is an all-female Liberal Arts institution in the heart of what's called the University City. In walking distance to Bennett is North Carolina Agricultural and Technical University (NCA&T), a co-ed research institution. It had a total undergraduate enrollment of 5515 with a gender distribution of 2840 male enrollment in 1976. Though I was on a female campus, there wasn't a shortage of male companionship. There was a saying on campus, NCA&T men could have a Bennett girlfriend before curfew, (Yes, Bennett had a curfew) and an NCA&T girlfriend after Bennett's doors locked. I soon figured out how to get around the timing issue and party.

My mother wanted me to attend college though she didn't go to college. She always furthered her education through classes and practical curriculums. Mom always took advantage of courses that broadened her knowledge in dressmaking and business. Dressmaking came naturally for her. She used this skill to help her and her family in their household expenses. She was a strong lady. Born and raised in the south, she later moved to New York for better employment opportunities. She worked as she could, taking jobs that paid little. Dressmaking always supplemented her income. There were times she held three and four positions to keep her family fed, clothed and the rent paid.

Mom instilled in me an intellectual thought-process of life. By this, I mean the ability to think things through. Mom, being a seamstress by trade could figure out how pieces of clothing fit together making a beautiful garment, without directions. She could figure out how one piece of fabric would look, connect, and how it would blend with another material. For example, she might consider how a silk blouse would coordinate with a fur collar. Her thought process was amazing. If this, then that.

It may seem simple, but this is a learned process that she instilled in my two brothers and me. It worked the following way:

- Decide what you want to do, stick to it. If it doesn't work the first time, figure what needs to happen and go forth. That's discipline.
- Don't sell yourself short. Find the combination that works. Maybe silk and fur won't work but, silk and wool would

professionally dry clean better. Think through the integrity of your project.

- After you go through all the garment makings, was it worth it? What will be the return on your investment?

- After considering the Return on Investment (ROI), is there anything you could do to give yourself a better performance? Money and time are invaluable. Could you reduce your time by reducing the number of buttons? Thinking through your tactics is vital. It's most important.

- How do you feel about your project? Did you accomplish what you wanted? Do you think you would change anything, if so, why?

My Mom instilled this problem-solving process in me and my brothers. She was raised with her 9 brothers and sisters. With so many people in the house, you had to figure things out on your own, then get confirmation for your efforts. The atmosphere was fast paced, so many people going in different directions. Mom was the youngest girl and often had to fend for herself, but she was never alone. She was very petite, standing only about 4 feet 11 inches, but she was tall in her stride for excellence and the use of imagination. She figured things out. If a project needed a part that she didn't have, she would try to make it, if she couldn't buy it.

She met my father. Dad was a New Yorker. They were together for about 25 years making their home between New York and Manchester before he was called to heaven.

Dad was a different story. He was an electronic engineer. His field dealt with circuit boards, transistors, fiber optics and such. His philosophy in life was to focus on what is essential. You can listen to your mother on how to dissect issues but maintain focus on what is necessary.

Dad was about 5 feet 11 inches tall, weighing around 240 pounds grey hair and a friendly smile. Dad wasn't flashy but always looked neat in his clothing. He had a calm demeanor and was easy going. He always tried to talk things out and was non-argumentative. Funny thing, Dad also was an auxiliary police officer but did not like confrontational issues. He instead would instead walk away than stand toe to toe and argue. Dad said people usually focus on another matter and not the real problem. He wanted to get to the root of the problem and focus on a solution.

Dad's circle of friends was small. He was an only child and felt many friends were not essential, but the chosen few were important. He placed a high value on his friends. With his idea on focus and mom's notion of the process working together, issues could be solved. They may not end the way you imagined them, but a solution is at the end of any question, struggle or problem.

I was in college and came home to Manchester for the summer. My dad and I went to get a sandwich at our favorite restaurant, "The Wedge Inn," where they served veal cutlet parmesan on hoagie buns. It was always easy to hold conversations over a meal. I told him about school and my social life. He was pleased my education was going well, but in my social life, he had questions. I expressed to him the guys I met and dated were OK but not special. I wanted someone special. Coming up empty. He told me to stop looking and enjoy life, the right guy would find me. "Just remember the lessons mom and I taught you and stay strong with your beliefs and standards, continue to embrace them. Make us proud".

Months later I told my dad someone special had come into my life. We talked for a while. Then he asked questions about the boyfriend. He wanted to know if he was good to me. Was he a hard worker? Would he make a good father? What were his parents like? Are you equally yoked in your spiritual beliefs? Do you have the same interest? Are you going to marry him? Was he going to ask? Was he helpful; was he kind; did he attend college, etc.? My father asked everything and made sure I had an answer. He wanted to know if I remembered and respected the teachings he and my mother instilled in me; and if I would instill them in my children as they did me. Several months after that talk Dad passed away.

## Missed Signs

My boyfriend Wade and I dated, and we eventually married. We settled in Chattanooga, Tennessee, where we were employed and began our family. Our first child was a girl named Janelle and later a son named Gary. I stopped smoking when I found out I was pregnant. I didn't smoke or drink during pregnancy, trying to give the children's growth and development a good foundation. Both were healthy children.

Janelle met all her benchmarks growing up, height, weight, motor skills, cognitive skills, and became an honor student in school. She made friends quickly and was involved in school and extracurricular activities, a healthy, average child. I still had a career, while Janelle was in school, and relied on our daycare support system, Kathy's Little Stars Day Care, to help fill the gaps. Wade and I became good friends with the directors and staff. Kathy's Little Stars was a place to help kids grow and learn, which reinforced our ideas on both Janelle and Gary becoming the best they could be. Both children were in scouting, which helped build their character and self-esteem. We, as parents, built them up, giving them hugs, kisses, praises, to boost their self-esteem. Then, friends entered the picture.

Kathy's Little Stars provided lifelong friendships for Janelle and Gary. Gary started the daycare at six weeks old and was their first infant in the infant department. They fell in love with my baby. Janelle was attending another daycare and started Kathy's Little Stars when she was potty trained, about 1-1/2 to 2 years old. When Janelle joined him, they gave her the same love and attention. There were two children named Ryan, a boy and a girl, in Janelle's class. Ryan, the girl, and Janelle became good friends, and to this day, they are the best of friends.

At home, Janelle had her room. It was nicely decorated, rose pink painted below the chair rail and wallpaper above the chair rail. The wallpaper had a cream background with large pink connecting bows and pink and white accessories. She also had a full-size bed, dresser, and desk for homework, lots of books and toys. When the room was picked up and cleaned, it was stunning. After my daughter spent time in the room, it looked like a tornado hit the place. Stuff was everywhere. Toys, clothes, papers, and books, were scattered all over the floor and bed. Janelle was about six years old. She didn't like picking up after herself in her room. She helped in other areas of the house, but not her place. I thought it was a phase.

I tried to work with her to help her understand, a dirty room wasn't acceptable. It didn't help. I punished her. The restrictions didn't seem to matter to her. I took away her music. She enjoyed the quiet. I took away her clothes. She was OK with wearing the same outfit. I took away privileges. She seemed pleased to stay home. I took away television, she read school books. I was at my wit's end. She wore me down. About a month passed, and she showed some progress but not entirely. I was exhausted, and I caved in and cleaned the room myself. In hindsight, this may have been the beginning of Janelle's distaste to keeping a tidy home.

Janelle entered the neighborhood elementary magnet school. She was a great student. She enjoyed participating in plays and received many awards from perfect attendance to most improved in math and being on the "Star" role.

She was excited to have Gary join her in the elementary school. She taught him the alphabet and how to read. She was a great big sister.

Soon it was time to graduate from elementary school, and Janelle's personality came out. She developed a desire to sing. We went on a quest to find a youth choir for her participation. The youth choir filled her time, along with scouting.

Janelle and Gary remained close during the school years. They had scouting organizations in common as a shared interest but, other activities took them in different directions, including high schools.

Janelle was in high school, and her grades dropped. Wade and I expressed to her how crucial it was for her to keep her grades up in her classes for graduation and college entry. Our expressions went in one ear and out the other. Two semesters went by, and Janelle received nothing higher than a "C." Ironically, the "C" was in voice class. Everything else was "D" or "F." I couldn't believe it. I told her, "I give up. I no longer care about your grades if you don't." From that point, it was up to her. The next semester the report card was all "F's." Instructors commented on her lack of interest in everything.

Conversely, her social life at school was booming. We explained to her it was going to be nearly impossible to get a chance for higher education in college if she continued earning such low grades. Instructors may not give her the benefit of the doubt to get better grades, since she disrespected their classes, school, and had an "I don't care attitude." She would have to apply extra effort.

# The Esteemed High School

Janelle thought the rules didn't apply to her (without consequences.) She didn't want to clean her room, and the privileges she lost didn't matter to her. I couldn't find anything that mattered to her. She followed none of the incentives or bribes, and she was content to live as a monk. She didn't view losing privileges as having consequences. Janelle was smart and would have had to do minimal studying to make "A's" and "B's" on assignments and tests. She chose not to apply herself. She couldn't see what she was doing to her future. Many a night, I cried for her to wise up. When you don't think rules apply to you, you have nothing to lose.

Junior year, something clicked. Junior year is the year students begin to look at colleges with their guidance counselors. Janelle's friends were buzzing with college decisions. She was trying to figure out what to do. The pressure was on, friends going to college, her family was well-educated, several aunts and uncles and her parents all had college degrees from associate degrees to doctorate degrees. Of over 15 cousins, more than half had college degrees from bachelor's degrees to doctorate degrees. I know those are sizable standards, but today's job market is influenced by education.

Now, Janelle is finding the rules did apply to her. Some of her instructors saw a difference in her attitude and were willing to work with her, giving compliance measures of working hard and steady. A race to complete high school was on. She made good progress in her junior year and realized a class she botched wasn't going to be offered again until the following year, after her expected graduation. The alternative year class meant she would be in high school another year. Her counselor suggested she transfer to a high school that had the courses she needed to graduate. I thought about saying no and let her take the consequences for her actions but, remaining in high school an additional year may have punished me instead of her.

It was finally the senior year. Janelle was in a new school, gaining new friends. Her guidance counselor recommended community and junior colleges to her. I'm not sure she considered them because they were too close to home. She wanted to be away from home, "Miss Independence." Instead of a 4-year plan, her college would have her on a 5 to 6-year plan, due to remedial and prerequisite courses. Making up for high school shortfalls, at a college is very expensive, and her student loans would have to cover the cost if she went that route. The cost of college would be her responsibility.

*I thought the issues with Janelle were typical youth, tween and teen issues. I had no idea they may have been connected to low self-esteem. I missed the signs of defiance, believing that rules do not apply to her; taking responsibility for her actions and possible outcomes, and fear of failure. Low self-esteem can affect anyone, and life situations can exacerbate our self-esteem, whether positively or negatively.*

*I'm sorry Janelle, I didn't associate your behavior with low self-esteem and therefore failed to specifically address your needs. I needed to help you become more self-assured and connect you to resources that could help raise your self-esteem.*

# Ms. Independence, On the Road to College

This chapter was hard to write. As a mother, you are the first protector of your child. While carrying the child in the womb, you are the protector, nurturer, and doctor. God is so amazing. He made the women's body an expansive unbelievable vessel. It moves everything, organs, intestines, and lungs out of the way so that the baby can grow and become the little human it is designed to be. God entrusted the mother with nurturing that allows this to happen.

Many understand the saying "mess with my child, you mess with me." It made me reflect on all it took to bring a child into the world. I had high-risk pregnancies. Bringing Janelle into the world was more stressful than most normal pregnancies. I had more doctor visits, exams, medicines, and care. I sat Janelle on a pedestal. I was afraid that something would happen to her because of my past stupidity, trying to be grown before I knew what being grown was. So, when someone came into her life that didn't appreciate her or had negative feelings or actions towards her, I was offended. I was a protective mom.

We spoiled Janelle, and at times, she did not play well with others. She wanted to be the one who "seemed to have it going on." She was a daddy's girl. Her daddy did not have her wish for anything. Not that she got everything she wanted when she wanted it. Soon after she wanted it, she got it though. Janelle getting what she wanted gave her the appearance on campus she was a princess. So much so, she gave herself the nickname Princess with the spelling Pryincess, go figure.

Before attending the Historically Black Colleges and Universities (HBCU) campus tours, she wanted to participate in Dudley's Beauty School in Greensboro, North Carolina, to become a hair stylist. They did not have campus dorms, which would have required her to live off campus in an apartment. Because of her schedule, she would have needed a car to get to and from school. As parents, we were not ready for her to have that level of independence. It seemed to be too much freedom and responsibility.

Instead, Janelle agreed to go to college. She said she wanted to attend an HBCU. She found one that felt comfortable to her, Scruggs College in Normal, Alabama. We met several of the administrators and some staff. Everything felt like a good fit. We were comfortable leaving her on move-in day. They had a famous choir, and the director spoke of scholarship money if Janelle auditioned and joined the choir. All was good. She loved to sing, and she was at an HBCU. She had some independence. We thought an excellent education with scholarship money was a good match.

Scruggs College was a good college in academics and promoted independence, as all colleges do. They had access to the best professors and choices for a social life. Janelle treated college and her freedom with new vigor. However, more energy was placed on social activities, than classroom interest.

It did not take long for Janelle to develop a social network. She found several young ladies and young men, with whom she became best friends. The friends were a very selective circle, who she remains friends with to this day.

Janelle also had particular thoughts on the classes she should attend. Those she wanted to take part in, she did, and others she decided not to participate. Her private hair salon opened, and she chose to style hair over attending class.

*We knew how this would end.*

The dorm would not permit a student-run hair salon. Janelle and her roommate were at odds, and Janelle wanted to move out. An on-campus apartment opened. Janelle applied, and she soon moved in. *(If I only knew what was about to come, maybe things could have been different.)*

Now that Janelle had her self-imposed selective independence, she was living large. She was in an apartment, only attending the classes she wanted. Room, board and a food plan were in her pocket. Living without parents and classes gave her time to have a full-time boyfriend, privacy, and a city without parents to interfere.

Then came Rashad. I'm not sure how she met Rashad but, she did. Janelle described Rashad as nice looking, smart, and having a football player build, not the stocky type but the slim fit type. He was a student at Scruggs College as well. Soon they hung out together. They enjoyed spending time together and had a few mutual friends. The next thing you know, he was a constant friend at her apartment and began staying overnight. Their relationship became closer, they fell in love. Together they probably said all the right things to each other.

Rashad could talk a good game. He could give answers to your questions as if he wrote your questions, he was able to read people. He was very smart, not only with book knowledge but also street sense.

# Ring, Ring

Rashad became Janelle's everything. It was more fun and meaningful to be with Rashad than attending the few classes she was attending. Together they became like Jack and Jill, Frick and Frack, and the sun and the moon. Where one was, so was the other. They were inseparable.

One day in May, Janelle called and told me I would be a grandmother. I was in shock and speechless. It took me a while to gain my voice and utter a sound saying, "What did you say?" I told her we had to talk face-to-face.

*I was shocked she decided to start a family. All the birth control at her disposal didn't make a difference. I realize just saying no can be a hard choice to make in the heat of passion. The alternative would affect her entire life.*

When she came home, we talked about the possibility of abortion, her plans for life, school, living, and raising a child with or without the father. Janelle didn't believe in abortion, so she was having the baby. Her life would happen regardless, she needed to find a good obstetrician and have all the testing done. Janelle had plans on continuing her education. Janelle wanted to live at home until she got on her feet. Rashad was meeting with an army recruiter, in Alabama, about joining the armed forces, so that she and the baby would have benefits. I got through it, and we were able to move forward.

Janelle returned to school. She enrolled in the summer session to try to gain as many credits as she could before the baby was to be born, knowing the next semester would be her hardest. Getting adjusted to having a family and studying would have its difficulties.

As August rolled around, Janelle called to say she was leaving school, it wasn't working out. My reaction was, No, No, No. I tried to be understanding, knowing what she was going through. I felt her life took a significant turn, starting a family, and now her education was taking a significant turn too. It hit me like a ton of bricks.

*Was Janelle headed in a downward spiral? It's hard enough trying to find a job or career to support yourself, and now she has a family with no education. Young people feel they can do it, but it may be difficult, much more difficult than attending classes.*

We talked, and she was positive about getting her life on track. She laid out her vision for her education, the hopes, and dreams for raising her baby and becoming self-supportive.

Wade and I went to help her clean out her apartment. We met her boyfriend, Rashad. We did not impress each other. I should have known then. Life would not be simple. We got her packed and moved home.

# And the Doorbell Rang

*I'm old school, part of the baby boomer generation. I grew up believing life has an order. First thing in life was to go to church, have a career, get married, have a family, buy a house, enjoy life and die. Following the path was easy.*

Janelle was getting adjusted to being home. The doorbell rang, and Rashad was on the other side with a suitcase. We said greetings and I invited him in. Yes, I invited him in. Looking back on it, I should have stepped outside and held the conversation. Rashad came in, Wade and I talked with him. I was under the assumption he was going to stay in Alabama until the baby was born and continue working. He told us he wanted to be closer to Janelle and her pregnancy. I couldn't argue with the logic. It was sweet although not practical. How were they going to eat? Where were they going to sleep? We talked for a while, and we learned he was a master of "the answer." He had an answer for everything, and it sounded good. We gave him the benefit of the doubt on some things. We figured he was young and still had to figure things out.

Rashad told us, he had plans on joining the armed forces, the army. He had spoken with several recruiters in Normal, Alabama and they referred him to a recruiter in Chattanooga. By entering the military, Janelle and the baby would have benefits to help them for life. He said when he and Janelle were married they would have a good start in life.

Janelle joined the discussion. She seemed puzzled to see him, yet happy. She finally had something in her life that was hers and was seemingly not going away. He came to be with her. She thought it was love. Our lives were changing before our eyes.

They did the deed, it was done, and she was pregnant. I guess it was OK for them to sleep together. I changed the rooms around to give them the basement bedroom. It had some privacy, more than upstairs, and sound reduction. I thought that would be a good thing, but it would later prove to be one of the biggest detriments of my life.

Rashad was making conversation over dinner one night. Wade asked how the recruitment was coming along. Rashad said, "It's not, they were lying to me, I'm not going to the army." Wade and I were waiting for basic training to start because we did not want to put pressure on him for a job search if basic was beginning the next week. We discussed him not having a job. He said he needed to get the lay of the land and he would get a job. We really needed for him to get a job. We, the parents, did not want to support the extra three people now in the household, (Janelle, Rashad, and baby-to-be.) I was adamant not to support Rashad. I thought it was stupid to quit a job with a baby on the way, move to a new city without a job and no viable way to contribute to the ongoing of a household; such as rent, food, water to wash the body or bathroom tissue.

Janelle and Rashad seemed to get along well. They talked, went on walks, and at times drove to Normal, AL. to visit friends and his family. All was good. They had an occasional argument but, solved the issues without much effort. Over the past week or two, they felt relaxed and settled into home life. Seeing them together, I felt, was probably the way they were in the college apartment.

*Fast forward.* The baby due date is getting closer, and he still has no job. I'm getting frustrated because I don't see the effort in finding one. Within walking distance from my home is one of the largest shopping centers in the state. Along with the mall stores, there are about 500 ancillary stores. If he applied to ten jobs a day, eventually someone will hire him. I think he wanted to skate. I guess Janelle planted it in his head that her parents would deal with her situation, being pregnant, and he could come to Chattanooga, and it would be OK.

Janelle has friends that have babies and live at home with their parents. Their parents seemed to be OK with their situations. I don't know for sure.

A long time ago a parent told me her child told her, in sad and trying times, the only thing parents would do was to holler, fuss, cuss, stop talking to her for a while and then be over it. I got the feeling that is what Janelle felt as well.

Rashad found it insulting that I asked him daily if he applied for or found a job. He would blow up and start fussing. He thought his fussing would shut me up. I gave it back to him word for word. I was not afraid. I stood toe to toe with him.

Mom: Rashad, how is the job hunting coming along?

Rashad: Nothing yet today.

Mom: Where did you apply?

Rashad: At the mall.

Mom: Where?

Rashad: (breathing heavy). The food court.

Mom: (not believing). Which restaurants?

Rashad: (getting mad). Why?

Mom: Just checking progress.

Rashad: Why?

Mom: Maybe I can make some suggestions. You need a job.

Rashad: I can find my own job.

Mom: Do it and prove it.

Rashad: I don't have to prove anything.

Mom: How are you going to provide for your family?

Rashad: I'm doing it now, aren't I?

Mom: Not for long in this house.

## Planting the Seed

Both families were now under one roof. Janelle was toward the end of her pregnancy, and I asked her if she and Rashad were going to get married. I think the idea had come across her mind again, now it was said out loud. She didn't know the answer. I don't know how often they discussed it before I asked but, now it's a topic of conversation.

Janelle didn't talk about a plan "B" after Rashad decided not to join the army. The army was her ticket toward real independence. I did not know how she saw her future.

We were sitting at the table, Janelle announces they are getting married. It seemed we were at the table on Monday and we were having a park wedding on Saturday. Rashad's mother is a minister living in Alabama, she was going to perform the marriage ceremony.

Saturday morning, we drove from Chattanooga to Normal. It was a lovely, simple park wedding in Alabama. Everyone seemed happy. Janelle and Rashad had no money. My husband and I gave them a night at a hotel for their honeymoon. Both families went to a restaurant for lunch to celebrate. I'm not sure if it was a wedding dinner, but it ended up that way. We paid for it all, (I felt) by default since we were parents of the bride. Rashad's family offered nothing to the celebration, not even the tip. It would have been nice for a contribution, a donation or a gift to the newlyweds, if not for lunch, then for the added expense of Rashad living with us. Monetary consideration would have been appreciated. I wondered, what are we getting into, blending the two families? We are not rich. We didn't have extra money for this. We wanted to see our daughter happy and would do almost anything not to disappoint her. Yes, she is spoiled.

I remember that sunshine blue-sky day in Alabama. The park has good memories. There were good memories after that but, as always, the bad memories outweigh the good ones. I am sorry I opened my big mouth, asking if they would marry, I planted the seed.

## What's a Mother to Do?

It wasn't easy watching my daughter navigate through life with so many variables. She was juggling the roles of wife, breadwinner, daughter, an independent woman, and impending mother. That's a lot for anyone, especially a person thinking she is grown but still has an air of immaturity. Young people think they know more than they do.

Janelle was impressionable and in love. She wanted to follow her husband. I think she wanted a marriage as stable as her parents. Her father and I had a happy marriage over 35 years, and still, we are in love. Our longevity is attributed to talking matters out and a willingness to stand united, even if one of us disagrees with the other.

I tried to give Janelle her space and not interfere in her relationship. They needed to grow as a unit. When she or he came to us with questions, we tried to give honest answers and backed them up with questions for their thought. We decided to instill TEAMwork. Expressing that they must work as a team because their individual lives were over was easy to say, but a hard concept for them to grasp. It seemed the transition from boyfriend to husband and girlfriend to the wife was a concept that had little meaning. For them, together meant together, and marriage meant they could sleep together legally in their parents' house.

Our house has a master suite downstairs, along with a den. When the doorbell rang that day, I cleaned most of my belongings out of the downstairs and gave that area to Janelle and Rashad. Now, it was a task to move my things and find new homes for them in the garage and upstairs. I did this to show I supported their family unit. The redecorating decision was an effort to give them and their marriage a chance. The bedroom was on the opposite end of the house from mine, giving each of us some privacy.

This arrangement worked for a while. The honeymoon period was short. Janelle and Rashad needed more room. It seemed to get on their nerves, being so close together. Rashad didn't have a job to go to, and she wasn't working either. The arguments started, or maybe this is how their relationship was in Alabama.

My husband and I discussed things and respected each other's opinion, even if it was different. We didn't raise our voices. Sometimes, we had to walk away and revisit the issue later to keep the respect of each other's opinion. Revisiting matters worked for us. We shared this method with Janelle and Rashad. They didn't or couldn't understand. Their way of whoever could talk the loudest (to get their point across) won the disagreement.

Rashad was no pushover. I learned from him, he grew up listening and watching his mother take abuse from his father. Rashad could suppress his anger. The stress of a new baby, no job, no income, new wife, new city, and living with the in-laws was a bit much. He could no longer suppress his real personality and expressed it the way his father expressed actions towards his mother. I never witnessed Rashad's physical abuse, but the verbal abuse was an eye-opener.

Janelle could stand her ground. She saw stable marriages all around her and knew arguing and fussing wasn't the way to solve problems. Janelle thought she had the upper hand. She was in her parents' house so it would be her way or the highway. Janelle was the first of her single parent friends to marry the child's father. Thinking this set her apart; she felt her marriage had a better chance of working.

One day suddenly, yelling started downstairs. Wade and I tried to stay out of it and let them work it out. It became louder and louder and moved upstairs. When this happened, Wade and I came forward to see what was going on. They had a heated argument over cleaning up. Janelle has an issue with cleaning up. She doesn't like to do it. Rashad felt the quarters were too tight not to clean up. She thought she was carrying the burden of living expenses (or her parents were) and he should make more of an effort. We told them to work it out, and most of all stop the yelling.

# You Pulled the Trigger

What is your trigger? You never know what it will be. I am a well-balanced person, I think. Even tempered, I thought, was my demeanor. I tried to stay out of their relationship and let them come together and work it out. It was hard.

This day, I don't know what happened, but the yelling started. Everywhere she walked, he was right behind her like she was his child. I didn't yell like that, and I'm her mother. The yelling started inside the house, then it was outside the home. It went back inside the house, then to the driveway. She started walking up the front walkway to go into the house. I came to the front of the house to see what was going on and saw the degradation. It was awful. Rashad was standing nose to nose with Janelle, yelling in her face, and she was just standing there taking it.

I walked up to him, he didn't stop. I asked him to stop. I told him to keep the issues inside the house. The neighbors didn't need to know why they were arguing. Was I trying to save face with the neighbors? Anyway, it was necessary for them to calm down and figure it out.

I couldn't believe Janelle. The one that could hold her own with anyone on the playground and anyone in the work office, letting him yell in her face like that. What was up with her? I figured he was her husband and she was trying to respect his opinion. She never, ever saw her dad and me argue like that. I felt so sorry for her. I told them to go inside, sit down and talk like adults. They went inside. The anxiety was still high, but they talked it out.

*I wanted to hurt him so badly. He was degrading my daughter. No one should or has the right to treat anyone like dirt. No one, the one who confessed to love you in front of God and witnesses, no one should treat you like dirt. What did he perceive her doing that made him mad? I bet it was something stupid she had no clue about doing. I tried to put myself in her place. What would I do? Would I stand and take the fussing and cussing in my face? I'd like to think not. I needed to build her self-esteem up, not tear it down.*

Domestic violence victims are five times more likely to end up dead if their abuser has access to a gun.

I don't own a gun. If I had one, I'd have gone for it. If I had no other option, it would be Rashad or me. A case study mentions femicide but, if a gun is present, it gives people an additional physical opportunity instead of using intelligence to solve a problem. The situation became intense.

As a young girl, my father taught me to shoot a gun. A very crucial lesson went along with that responsibility. His teaching was never to aim a firearm at someone to scare them, only point the gun at them to shoot and destroy them.

I'm not pro or con, for or against guns. I just think there is a better way, other than guns, to solve a problem.

*I was not able to judge if the argument would remain verbal or turn physical.*

*At that point, I was trying to be an adult, think through the situation as my mother taught me. My father also would have been proud, focus. My thoughts went to Landen, the unborn baby. What would happen to him if his family dynamics fell apart?*

Rashad was becoming a big problem. Our home felt like his name was on the mortgage, and we were the guests. His personality was becoming too large for my house. Bullying in my presence, in my home, he was disrespectful, period.

On the one hand, I wanted Janelle to be a happy wife and mother. On the other hand, I wanted Rashad out of her and the baby's life. She had to make the choices for her life. I was there to support her and listen. I tried to keep my opinions silent, I WANTED HIM OUT OF HER LIFE.

He pulled the trigger with his domineering attitude and started the marriage destruction bullet in motion, toward Domestic Violence.

Domestic Violence is when an intimate partner abuses the other in areas of sexual, physical, verbal, psychological, emotional turmoil, or a combination of any battering. Bullying and gaslighting, discrediting the partner by making others think they are crazy, are also used to maintain psychological power and control over their partner.

*I don't know if this is a domestic violence relationship. I know it isn't a loving relationship. It seems to be a weird dependence on both parts. My mind says its domestic violence, but I don't want to believe my mind. Not my child.*

## Not Picture Perfect

My family is an accommodating family. The things our children want of us, if it's not too farfetched, we try to do. When Rashad came to the house, we wanted to accommodate him because of Janelle. We asked him about work ethics. Rashad responded that he works, and he knows he must provide for his family. It seemed, though, he needed to work when he wanted to work to accomplish his desires. I had no desire to have a young man sleeping with my daughter, living in my house, and not contributing to the household; not even buying soap to take a shower. Was this how he was raised?

Sometimes I think Janelle gave him false concepts of her family dynamics. Janelle was proud of her parents and their accomplishments. We were not rich, but God saw that we had the things we needed. He even let us have joys. We worked hard to achieve some nice things and go on vacations. Since Janelle was able to get her father and myself to meet her wants, I think she felt Rashad was now an extension of her and he should be able to enjoy the same. Janelle's thoughts of Rashad as an extension of her was a misnomer. It will not happen. As parents, we supplied a roof, food, water, and some cash. I wondered if his family was helping them financially. We saw no help. Landen's paternal grandmother, aunt, great uncle, and cousin attended his baptism in Chattanooga. They haven't returned to Chattanooga, called, written, or texted since. Rashad received help from Janelle through us, until he got a job with an auto parts store. Aid lasted too long from us, and the auto parts job didn't last long enough.

Janelle was proud of her family. She always said she wanted her family to work. When things were good, they were first rate. When things were bad, they were horrible. I had watched one of the crime scene stories on TV. The episode had a scene where the killer husband went through a photo album and scratched out the wife's face from all the pictures. Later the wife was found dead.

While I was cleaning the house one day, I found a large white envelope of photos. The photos were of Janelle, Rashad, and Landen. The faces of Janelle were all scratched out. I was in shock. In the TV show, the investigators used the pictures to convict the husband for killing the wife. Was my daughter's life in danger or was she just hated by her husband? I didn't sleep a wink for a few days after that. I was scared for my daughter.

*I'm still trying to figure out if this is a domestic violence relationship. I know something is not right. Janelle and Rashad are like oil and water. They are not mixing well together. I remained silent because I didn't know what to do. I prayed and prayed that an answer would come soon before someone got hurt.*

# Notes from Mom

Am I a momzilla or just a concerned mom? In my mind, I've taken Rashad in a boxing ring and laid into him. When the bell rang, he couldn't get up. I beat him so bad. Janelle had about the same bout. I slapped her so much her face had permanent hand marks. She realized the relationship wasn't a good one for her.

Since Janelle and Rashad were married, they had lived with me and moved into an apartment. Janelle has been back and forth over several months depending on the status of their relationship.

Last weekend Janelle spent it at the apartment with Rashad. Wade and I just shook our heads. This week, about a month later, they go out for a weekend then come back over to our house. They picked up the baby and took the baby back over to the apartment.

I guess love or stupidity wins out. Wins out over what? I pray there is not a next time of moving back and forth between home and the apartment, or at least, next time there is no bloodshed. I must admit blood is always on my mind and my mind hasn't been clear in a long time. I believe my hair falling out was because of the turmoil.

My stress level was high. I'm dealing with it by myself and absorbing work to the fullest. Wade was doing the same. We draw strength from each other. I give him an ear full and many tears. We consoled each other. Still, we are sitting on the sideline watching the happenings, hoping and wishing for something better.

The only way I know to protect my daughter is to be there for her. I believe deep down inside, she knows her relationship is souring. I can listen and give her a place of refuge when she needs it.

*Isaiah 40:29*

*He gives power to the faint and strengthens
the powerless.*

# **Down & Dirty Notes**

_____

_____

_____

_____

_____

_____

_____

_____

_____

_____

_____

_____

_____

_____

_____

# Chapter 2

# Learning Survival Techniques

*Every seed must rise through dirt to enjoy the sunshine."*
**Matshona Dhliwayo**

# Down & D.I.R.T.Y. to 180° Technique

## AMEND THE DIRT, and YOU CAN TURN IT 180°

Down & Dirty to 180° is a technique used to take one from low self-esteem, feeling down on themselves or an unhealthy situation and turning it around 180°.

Sometimes our lives throw us a curveball and treat us as if we are the lowest of the low, low like dirt, something that someone can walk all over.

The Down & D.I.R.T.Y. to 180° technique can help turn that around. It stands for "***Discipline, Imagine, Realizing, Tactics***, *and* ***You***, *turning it around.*"

Realizing any new technique or approach takes time to accomplish, you will become a better you with a celebrated acknowledgment of focus, goals, desires, roadmaps, and strengths.

Janelle used this technique and applied it to her life. After making realizations and changes, she was able to turn her life around.

Janelle settled down, evaluated her life and the direction in which it was moving. She felt her life had to change. Janelle was unsure if the abuse she was feeling of psychological, emotional, and verbal torment would also fall on Landen. She was ready for a change.

## Discipline Yourself

You can only truly change yourself, not others. To improve, you must want to change. Some feel the way they live is perfect and there is no need to change. The aggressor in a relationship may feel they are the "right" one. It is their way or the highway. This thinking can inflict pain on loved ones and those around them in marriage, the office, and in life.

Change can happen overnight for some things or slower for most things. If you want to stop smoking cigarettes, would you consider buying them more, less or the same? If you wanted to lose weight, would you go to all you can eat buffets? If you wanted to stop mistreating someone, would you go to boxing matches or watch street brawls on TV? Not to say anything is wrong with boxing. It has its place, but it is an aggressive sport. Change your mindset and change you.

You may have to change your environment. The environment can have a role in self-discipline. Recognizing the signs that motivated or triggered anger could be the beginning. Symptoms such as the hairs standing up on the back of the neck, a change in breathing, seeing the blood rise from the chest, ears, and face can show an environmental change is needed. When these feelings come upon you, focus and give a positive reaction. You may have to change your environment, re- move yourself for a moment and collect your thoughts. Changing your thoughts can change your response. Remember to transform; you must start the process and live the process.

Rashad seemed to be the aggressor and needed to curtail his emo- tions to handle situations in a more acceptable manner. He and I were talking one day. He hinted a desire to change. I shared with him some of my colorful past. He asked me, "How did you change?" My re- sponse was, "Change your mindset and change you. Remember, to be changed, you must start the process and live the process. You have to treat it like a bad habit you want to kick."

Rashad once told me he felt the deck was stacked against him. He was married but living in his in-law's home, under their rules. His wife was with him but still under her parent's umbrella. He was his own man and wasn't allowed to be "Rashad free" because of his living sit- uation. He couldn't fully relax, and be the master of his own castle, and run his household the way he wanted.

There was no money. The Christmas seasonal work had come and gone. Rashad wasn't working, and Janelle was on him to find a job to support his family. Did he feel, since he was living with the in-laws, they needed to support his family? Well, the in-laws, along with Janelle, wanted him to at least try to find a job. It was January the baby was just born. Janelle couldn't work yet. What were they going to do? The lack of money was becoming problematic. Rashad was feeling the heat. He and Janelle began to argue more. One day he got so mad that he pulled her glasses off her face, bent them in half, broke them, and threw them across the room. No self-control. Rashad could have continued doing as he had done and walked outside to distance himself from the conversation. He now must buy another pair of glasses. He had no insurance and no job. Janelle also could have walked away and cooled down before tempers escalated.

Focus on the change you want to make and begin the process.

Janelle could give as good as she got. She could stand toe to toe with Rashad in arguing. Janelle had to focus on walking away and calming down. The more she did this, she began to discipline herself to change. Janelle argued less and less. She figured it wasn't worth it. The longer she interacted, the longer the episode lasted. Janelle disciplined herself. Realizing the actions, it took, not arguing and walking away, changing the environment, calmed the situation down. She found it difficult.

Janelle never received a new pair of glasses from Rashad.

## Imagine the Outcome

As young people, we imagine what our life will look like when we get older. We would have the job of our dreams, a big house, maybe with a pool, beautiful furnishings and a very nice sports car, perhaps a convertible. Young girls imagine their ideal husband, that's well connected and resourceful. Our imaginations keep us interested in possibilities of our life's outcomes. We navigate to the positives, the good life. Reality still must be faced.

Some young people can't imagine the life mentioned above. They are in a cycle of torment that has not been shattered. What they see is what they do or expect. They repeat the aggression, and if the aggression cycle remains, they too can become abusers or seek those that abuse. The cycle must break at some point.

If working on the marriage, at some point, you must decide on your options. The first option is whether to stay in the union and option two is to get out of the marriage. Both options require a lot of thought and self-reflection to come to a decision. Weighing your options is as important as continuing to work on the marriage. If the marriage stays together, you know the story that's being told. If the union separates and divorce is pending, that's also a familiar story with more unfamiliar storylines in it. Whenever deciding, consider your goals, and you must weigh the potential outcomes. Marriage is no different.

Rashad told me his father abused his mother. He would watch his mother get slapped across the room, and he couldn't do anything about it. I don't know if Janelle knew about the abuse. They should have discussed how they were raised, their expectations, having children and how they wanted to raise them would impact their decision-making. Rashad already had one son, Mark, by a former girlfriend. He took part in raising him until he moved with Janelle. Janelle felt she should become the financial advocate for his son. She wanted Mark to know his father cares. She would send him money, from her paycheck, and small gifts. Janelle and Rashad's marriage was an unevenly yoked relationship.

Janelle always stated she wanted her marriage to work. I believe she tried. Time after time she went back into the eye of the storm. She had to learn that it's two in marriage and both parties must want the marriage to work for it to work. That was her goal, and she was putting her best foot forward. It is a fact that people go back into the abusive situation seven times before completely separating from the situation.

If Janelle leaves the marriage, decisions concerning Landen become paramount as, partial custody, full custody, weekend visitation, adjustment time and more. Was Rashad going to agree with decisions made? Was he going to honor them?

*My goal for Janelle had an order to it as well. She was to finish college, get a career established, save some money, and become as financially independent as she can, do some international travel, get married, set goals for herself, and start a family. These were my goals for her. (She may or may not have set goals for herself. Life comes as it comes is her philosophy, and she will deal with it as it comes.) It is hard to set goals when you wait for life to happen, being reactive instead of proactive. Being proactive should be primary. Set your goals and growth will occur. Your life might be ready for achievement.*

*Thinking back, Janelle set goals to attend an HBCU, have a high paying job, get her driver's license, get a car, and she accomplished those goals. When she set the goal to make her marriage work, she thought she would succeed. Problems continued to arise.*

## Realizing the Return on Your Investment

Perhaps you've heard the term or phrase Return on Investment, ROI. We have many investments in our lives, and at some point, we should evaluate them. Maybe we put them in a spreadsheet and think about them or decide if we need to continue putting time and effort into them. Marriage is a huge investment. From the moment you say, "I do" and "until death do you part" you are investing in your life with another. What do you want your return to be? A happy and fruitful life, one with a prosperous career, loving, faithful spouse and happy, well-balanced loving children, is a return on your investment some would love to have.

The return on investment involves life as you see it and life as you want it. If you want more, donating more time to understand your investment will deem valuable for long-term life decisions The ROI is what you make it. Trying to change another person can be fruitless, but you can understand another person and decide, if the relationship is worth what you are putting into it, the return.

Rashad had smoked marijuana in the past. Occasionally, he would smoke it again. Janelle says she never smoked or tried to participate in the activity. Rashad had some pot at the house. Janelle asked him to get rid of it. She didn't want it around Landen or her parents' house. He said no, he would smoke it outside and it wasn't bothering anything. She resisted drugs around her or the baby. An argument started and, before you know it, the yelling and screaming were getting louder. He tried to put his foot down, and she wasn't having it. It almost got physical. My husband had to break it up before it escalated.

Later Rashad asked Wade, "How do you make them listen and mind you?" Wade told him, "You must work together. It's not only one way to do things, compromise and again work together to work it out." By working on the relationship, you are investing in your marriage. The more time and energy you spend, the better and greater the understanding of your return will be.

Janelle always said, "I want my marriage to work." She had several friends that started their families without being married. The young ladies invested in the boyfriends in hopes for marriage. Some had more than one child by the same boyfriend, maybe trying to solidify the relationship, but there was no marriage. The return on investment was high in having beautiful children but low on marriage. Janelle was pregnant before marriage, then she and Rashad tied the knot. She was elated when Rashad wanted to marry her. The time and effort Janelle put into the relationship benefited her. Commitment for a life partner meant they were in love, she invested wisely, she thought.

*I'm not sure Janelle and Rashad knew what marriage was, what it really meant. I say this because after the "I do," the relationship seemed to change. It appeared he wanted the "man is the master of the house and the wife obeyed the master" type of home. She wanted a 50/50 relationship. They had two very different ideas on marriage.*

Janelle needed to invest in paying attention to Rashad's methods and desires. The relationship he wanted was one she glossed over. She saw it through rose-colored glasses. She didn't take it for what it was. They both needed to invest in one another for the best return.

## Tactic Implementation

Implementation of tactics is the process that turns your ideas into actions to achieve your goals. Take your plans off the shelf and put them into action. If you want to grow and change your future, you must improve your current environment, (the way you're doing things now). If you're going to stay the same as you are now, then keep on doing what you're doing. To implement or to put into practice new actions is the way to growth.

Success needs a roadmap. As you are planning for new growth, take time to think about how to get there. A map for success would be a guide to keep tactics on track. You can access the direction of your goals to see if any changes would be beneficial. The roadmap doesn't guarantee you will achieve your goals but will give you a guide to stay on a path to achieve your goals. Implementing your plan will provide you with the "why," "why not" and "what" you are going to do to achieve your goal. The tactics used will give you the "how," "where" and "when" you are going on your path.

Now that you can see success on your path, life has a way of derailing the best-made plans. You must own the decisions you make. Taking responsibility for your actions is what you can control. You cannot control the actions of others.

Begin your action plan:

- Own the things you do. Evaluate and decide if another plan of action is needed.

- Communicate with those who are needed for your plan's success. They can help. Remember, it's your plan. You know the results you want. Getting guidance from someone may prove beneficial if trying to achieve goals in unfamiliar areas. Evaluate the help.

- Day-to-day activities can consume your time. Try to block out planning time for yourself either daily, or weekly. Keep in touch with your short and long-term goals.

- Planning can become overwhelming. Sometimes we have such a long list of things we want to change, we don't know where to start. Look at your list and group ideas together. Some parts of the list may be accomplished while completing other parts.

- Start with something small; once achieved, you will be proud of your accomplishment and encouraged to finish the plan.

- Share your goals with other important people in your life. It will help you to be accountable to yourself and to others who know what you want to achieve. They can cheer and support you along the way.

Review your plan and hold yourself accountable for the current and final results. You can have someone keep you, or you can face yourself in the mirror and hold yourself accountable. You can write your plan down, note it in your phone, send an email to yourself, or however you need to keep track of your goals and how you are progressing. Create milestones in your plan. If you need to reset the benchmark, and move the completion date, continue to keep track and don't lose the momentum.

Accountability may motivate and improve your success plan. You will still need tools, to implement the program. Hold yourself responsible for getting what you need for success.

Ask yourself questions:

- How committed are you to the plan?
- How are you going to motivate yourself?
- What roadblocks do you have to avoid?
- Have you inquired about resources that can help you achieve your goals?
- Do you have access and control of all the elements to make the change?

Some answers to these questions may take more consideration than others. Be sure to think strategically to give yourself the best chance of success. One thing will lead to another. Some may need resources, both physical and financial, to achieve their goals. Do you have them ready, if required?

Change your plan as needed. It is your plan. Don't make it easy, make it significant and realistic. It is you that's wanting to grow. You may need to establish a scorecard and implement a reward system. All growth is up to you.

Ways your actions can be derailed, or survivors may be afraid that:

- They will lose their children.
- The abuser may harm pets.

- Their batterers will kill them if they leave.

- The violence will increase, based on past experiences.

- There is a lack of resources, financial, transportation, food, clothing.

*Janelle moved between our house and living in an apartment with Rashad. When she realized her marriage, her life, and Landen were needing to separate from Rashad, she made a to-do list. On Janelle's list, she first needed to get some rest and start with a clear mind. She desired to make copies of important papers to keep in a safe place. She gathered the paperwork and made copies at the post office on her way over to my house. Later, she needed to do volunteer hours at Landen's school to keep him enrolled. Rashad was not interested in the required parental participation in the daycare. She also was job hunting. Rashad had not worked steadily since moving to Chattanooga. Janelle needed to work. Both activities, volunteering, and working were vital to her livelihood. Janelle asked her dad and me to do volunteer hours while she continued to job hunt. It all worked out.*

It seems we must consider so much with tactics. It may be overwhelming. If you can see yourself moving to a better situation, you are already on your way.

Janelle asked Wade and me to work with her and be available for Landen while she was in transition. We were Team Janelle.

# You for You

You must learn to celebrate you for you. You are a culmination of the choices you have made in life. If you can rejoice, by saying yay, or the most, by having a party, stand up and give yourself a hand. You are alive, make changes and become a better you. Acknowledge your strengths and limitations. Take pride in your abilities and accomplishments. Feel good about yourself. None of us are perfect. We are what we are because of the choices that we've made and, if we don't like what we have become, it is up to us to make a change for the better. Take pride in yourself, you've come this far and survived.

Take inventory of yourself and be knowledgeable. You can't fix what you don't know to fix. We all have challenges on which we improve. The key is to acknowledge the problem and decide how to address it, but not to dwell on it, then move on.

One of the ways strengths and limitations can be acknowledged, is to make a list of them. You can find your strengths by deciding what you are good at without effort. There are things you are good at that you may not know you're good at, because they are so natural to you, such as photography or grilling.

You can find your limitations in the same way. Consider the things that are difficult for you. Being lazy and sloppy are limitations.

The following page is set up to do just that. In one column list your strengths and in the other your limitations. We are fast to list our limitations or weaknesses, and our strengths or strong points may come to us a little slower. Try to write 10 in each column. If the strength column presents a challenge, think of the positive's others may have said to or about you over the years.

Examples of Janelle's strengths include:

- You are beautiful when, working, teaching, and playing with children.

- You have a beautiful smile that encourages others.
- You enjoy sharing and inspiring others with kind words and encouraging messages.
- Janelle has a natural charisma to get children moving, to put together a play.
- In the age of selfies, Janelle takes pretty pictures of herself and friends and posts them on the Internet.
- She looks happy in her photos.
- I've seen her approach a child that didn't want to get out of his seat, walk them the dance floor and dance.
- She can persuade children to go to bed by reading them a story.
- She has a gift of gab and voice inflection.

I have listed what I perceive as some of Janelle's strengths to inspire and encourage you. Take time to think about your own strengths and gifts and record them on the Strengths and Limitation Chart at the end of this chapter.

Nobody makes long-term changes overnight. Expectations of yourself or others can be realistic or unrealistic. It may take weeks, months and maybe years to change behavior. Don't let that discourage you. Give it your best. If the change takes longer than you expect, or the time limit you have set for yourself, remember to be realistic. Unrealistic expectations can derail progress. Stick with it and work through it. You can get results.

- An example of a realistic goal can be to train and run a 5K race by the end of the year.
- An unrealistic goal may be to learn to fly a plane and fly to Alaska this weekend.

Stay focused on how to achieve your goal, tracking your progress, and learning from your failures.

You will never be perfect. Those around you will never be perfect. Perfection is a Hollywood script. Our lives are not perfect. Concentrate on accomplishments and avoiding missteps. You can take baby steps. Decide on small goals that are attainable and work toward making the changes. Learn from your mistakes and consider them a tool to move you forward by not repeating them.

Getting to know yourself can be scary. It isn't just about knowing your strengths and limitations, but also opening yourself up to new opportunities, new thoughts, trying out something new, new viewpoints, and new friendships. Learning what you offer others, or the world can be daunting.

Learning things new to us, things we haven't thought of yet, or haven't considered is how we can become the person we want to be. It takes trial and error, risk and courage to step out of your box. Knowing the new you is based on the NEW you. Don't base the achievements you gained on the old you. You are becoming a new you. Keep adjusting your self-image and self-esteem to reflect the new you and not the you of the past.

Now stop comparing the new you to the old you and stop comparing yourself to others. You are you and the only person to compare or compete with you is you. Changing you takes time and effort. Be patient. It will happen if the determination is applied. Get ready for the NEW YOU.

| Strengths | Limitations |
|---|---|
| 1. | 1. |
| 2. | 2. |
| 3. | 3. |
| 4. | 4. |
| 5. | 5. |
| 6. | 6. |
| 7. | 7. |
| 8. | 8. |
| 9. | 9. |
| 10. | 10. |

*Joshua 1:9*

*I hereby command you: Be strong and courageous; do not be frightened or dismayed, for the Lord your God is with you wherever you go.*

# **Down & Dirty Notes**

# Chapter 3

# The Power of
# Persuasion

*"Dirt is dirt, and we've all got it no matter where we come from. I'm not sure Christ sees one kind of dirt as dirtier than another. One thing is for sure: His blood is able to bleach any stain left by any kind of dirt."*
***Beth Moore***

# The Cycle of Domestic Violence

The entire cycle could take place in a day or longer. It has three phases:

1. **Tension Phase**- This is where tension builds over issues such as money, children, or jobs. The tension starts small and usually escalates to physical abuse.
2. **Acute Battering**- This begins with unpredictable behavior, as tension peaks and the physical abuse starts.
3. **Honeymoon Phase**- This happens when the abuser exhibits remorse after the abusive behavior. They try to convince you there is no reason to leave the relationship.

These cycles can happen repeatedly. It may be the reason victims stay in the relationship with the promise of the abuse not happening again, the honeymoon phase.

## Tension Phase

Janelle asked Rashad for shopping money to buy Landen shoes

and clothing. Rashad said, "Let your parents take care of clothes and daycare." An argument started.

## Battering Abuse started

He told Janelle he needed to go to the mobile phone store. She asked if he should go to the mobile phone store since he could not buy clothing for Landen? He told her to get out of the apartment.

## Honeymoon Phase

Realizing money was tight, he asked Janelle to come home.

## Can You Identify **Actions in the Cycle**?

_____

_____

_____

_____

_____

_____

_____

_____

_____

_____

# Power and Control Wheel

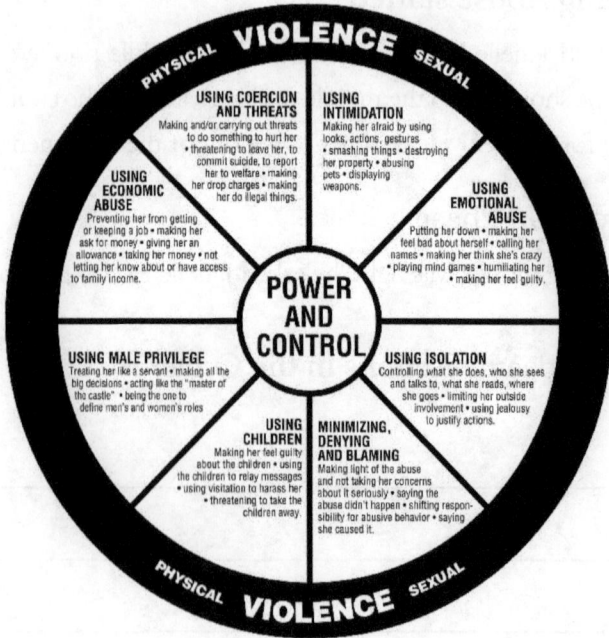

PHYSICAL **VIOLENCE** SEXUAL

**USING COERCION AND THREATS**
Making and/or carrying out threats to do something to hurt her • threatening to leave her, to commit suicide, to report her to welfare • making her drop charges • making her do illegal things.

**USING INTIMIDATION**
Making her afraid by using looks, actions, gestures • smashing things • destroying her property • abusing pets • displaying weapons.

**USING ECONOMIC ABUSE**
Preventing her from getting or keeping a job • making her ask for money • giving her an allowance • taking her money • not letting her know about or have access to family income.

**USING EMOTIONAL ABUSE**
Putting her down • making her feel bad about herself • calling her names • making her think she's crazy • playing mind games • humiliating her • making her feel guilty.

**POWER AND CONTROL**

**USING MALE PRIVILEGE**
Treating her like a servant • making all the big decisions • acting like the "master of the castle" • being the one to define men's and women's roles

**USING ISOLATION**
Controlling what she does, who she sees and talks to, what she reads, where she goes • limiting her outside involvement • using jealousy to justify actions.

**USING CHILDREN**
Making her feel guilty about the children • using the children to relay messages • using visitation to harass her • threatening to take the children away.

**MINIMIZING, DENYING AND BLAMING**
Making light of the abuse and not taking her concerns about it seriously • saying the abuse didn't happen • shifting responsibility for abusive behavior • saying she caused it.

PHYSICAL **VIOLENCE** SEXUAL

DOMESTIC ABUSE INTERVENTION PROGRAMS
202 East Superior Street
Duluth, Minnesota 55802
218-722-2781
www.theduluthmodel.org

The Power and Control Wheel developed by Domestic Abuse Intervention Project of Duluth, Minnesota, gave titles to the techniques abusers used to control their victims. Each of the eight titles lists several ways the abuser could use to gain power. The idea of gaining power is to keep power and control at their discretion.

The abuser can use one or more of these techniques at a time. Domestic Violence comes in more ways than one can count. The tactics used can change one's perspective, demeanor, thoughts, actions, beliefs and so much more.

It is crucial for the abused to find a line of communication, a journal, a confidante at work, some way to document what is happening in their lives.

The controller probably won't want this information made public, unless they are telling the story.

Expressing what goes on in the house to someone else may make the abuser feel out of control and more violent.

The survivor can call 911.

# Janelle's Stories

## Intimidation:

- Making her afraid by using looks, actions, and gestures.
- Smashing things.
- Destroying her property.
- Abusing pets.
- Displaying weapons.

**STORM**

On Saturday afternoon Rashad was texting Buffy. Janelle did not know Buffy.

Janelle: "Who is she?"

Rashad: "Mind your "f*****g" business. I'm going out to see Buffy, and it doesn't matter what you think. You go out with guys."

Janelle: "Like who?"

Rashad: "Trevor."

Janelle: "Are you kidding, you've gone out with Trevor, we've both gone out with Trevor and other friends as well. But, who is Buffy?"

They took the heated disagreement outside for the world to hear.

I would have liked to have been a bird in the tree the night Rashad got in Janelle's face, right in her face, nose to nose up close and personal. If a breath could be stolen for another breath, someone would be dead, that's how close he was.

The foul-mouthed Rashad was laying it on thick, talking about her family and how, every time there is an argument, Janelle calls her family.

Rashad: "Call your f*****g father and while you're at it you can f**k him too as well as suck his d**k, f**k him, you and your whole family."

Janelle started packing. She did not plan to stay with Rashad that night.

Rashad: "You're not taking s**t out of the apartment."

He took her suitcase, walked and threw the bag in the dumpster.

Rashad: "If you want it, go and get it."

She did. On the way back from the dumpster she saw him slash all four of her car tires. Yes, all four.

Janelle goes back to the apartment building and goes upstairs to use the neighbor's phone. She calls the police. As she is on the phone, Rashad comes in yelling at the neighbor.

Rashad: "Get the stupid b***h out of your apartment."

Neighbor: "Janelle, stay calm and take care of your business."

Four police cars showed up. Rashad was still carrying on with his foul mouth and derogatory language. He ended up getting arrested for disorderly conduct. Sunday was Father's Day and most of the day, he spent in jail.

Janelle gets a call from Rashad's sister Carla. Carla is not nice.

Carla said, "I hate you, I never liked you, I wouldn't pee on you if you were on fire and no water was around. I don't wear the tattoo I am my brother's keeper for nothing, and I never want to hear from you again."

Janelle breaks down and cries, then deletes her from her friend list on Facebook.

Janelle gets a call from Julia, Rashad's mother. She asked for the church pastor's phone number and hangs up. There is one more call to be expected, and that's from the grandmother.

## Can you identify acts of **Intimidation?**

_____

_____

_____

_____

_____

_____

_____

_____

_____

_____

_____

## Emotional Abuse:

- Putting her down.
- Playing mind games.
- Making her feel bad about herself.
- Calling her names.
- Making her think she's crazy.
- Humiliating her.
- Making her feel guilty.

### ONE UPPER

I was talking to Wade, and some new things came out of the conversation. Wade had been acting strange but trying to cover it up. Clearly, something was on his mind. I spoke with him to get his feedback on a conversation with Janelle.

Janelle called me crying and demanded answers.

Janelle: "Mom do you have breast cancer?"

Mom: "No, where did that come from?"

Janelle: "I was talking and arguing with Rashad."

Well, Rashad threw this in her face.

Rashad: "I know more of your family secrets than you do."

Janelle: "Rashad told me, Dad came to him crying and told him, Mom may have breast cancer and don't say anything to Janelle about it."

What Rashad didn't say, is that Wade was trying to talk to him about caring for the loved ones in your life. One way to do that is to try and shield them from bad news that could hurt them.

Janelle was pregnant at the time this came up. Her pregnancy was difficult along with her marriage, and she didn't need to know about this before the result of the biopsy.

The test, the biopsy came back negative.

I apologized for not talking to her, but having a negative biopsy, I just wanted to put it behind me.

Wade said he had something to share with me. He received a text message from Rashad belittling him for his parenting skills with Janelle, and how spoiled she was.

## Can you identify any **Emotional Abuse?**

_____

_____

_____

_____

_____

_____

_____

_____

_____

_____

_____

## Isolation:

- Controlling what she does, who she sees and talks to, what she reads, and where she goes.
- Limiting her outside involvement.
- Using jealousy to justify actions.

### Kill Joy

When will my daughter stop hurting? Today is her birthday. Rashad wished her a happy birthday at 7:30 this morning. She had meetings and work to attend, then a funeral.

During this time Rashad went to Alabama to help his sister with her car, so he said. Today is Friday, and he doesn't work on Saturday. He said he would be back when Janelle was finished with her daily duties.

It's 11:30pm, and he still isn't back. What is this? She said she came back over my house to finish a school paper and is now sitting in my living room crying. Her feelings are hurt. She always tries to make sure he has a good time whether it's going to a club or enjoying his birthday cake.

When will she learn? You know, either she will one day decide, she won't be stepped on anymore and kick him to the curb, or her feelings will always be hurt. I think he does this on purpose. He knew she would not call his sister, after the last time concerning the incident on Father's Day.

Remember, Janelle found where he was texting a girl in Alabama, an old girlfriend. While in Alabama he said he was on his way back when she called, but Rashad was computing on Facebook, so she knew he was lying. Anyway, how did he get to Alabama without a car and can't halfway get around Chattanooga without Janelle or is this his pitiful way? I say he is a user and he doesn't care for anyone but himself, very selfish.

Janelle probably felt more isolated than ever. He was jealous of her special day and left her. He kept her mind focused and occupied on him and his return thus limiting her outside involvement.

## Can you identify any **Isolation?**

_____

_____

_____

_____

_____

_____

_____

_____

_____

_____

_____

_____

## Minimizing, Denying, and Blaming:

- Making light of the abuse and not taking her concerns about it seriously.
- Saying the abuse didn't happen.
- Shifting responsibility for abusive behavior.
- Saying she caused it.

### THE SLAMMER

It was a regular night at my house. Everyone finished watching TV upstairs and getting ready to turn in. It was lights out and quiet. Suddenly, Janelle comes running upstairs crying and yelling. Rashad was right behind her. They were fussing, cussing, screaming, and carrying on. It woke Wade and me. We jumped up and ran to the living room to find out what was going on.

Janelle was talking through her tears that Rashad wouldn't leave her alone, he kept getting in her face. She was trying to protect herself and get him off her. He kept coming at her, she was trying to defend herself.

Rashad was saying, "She laid her hands on me and I was protecting myself. I told her, if you touched me again, I will call the police on you and report you." He said, "She pushed me." He called the police. Three police cars showed up at my house. They took information and arrested my daughter on domestic violence charges. My daughter was handcuffed and placed in the back of a police car and taken to jail.

Rashad got his things from downstairs and boldly walked out my front door with a bounce in his step. A bounce that said, "Yeah, I did it." One of the officers asked if they were married and how long? When he found the answer to be yes and 9 months, he offered the opinion, she should divorce him, soon. That it was a volatile relationship that would probably escalate to nothing good such as more jail time or death.

Sometime went past and Janelle and Rashad began to communicate again. Janelle forgave him for this action, and they tried to work things out.

Rashad trivialized the arrest by telling Janelle, "If you hadn't touched me by pushing me off you, I would have never called the police. You were responsible for being arrested and that being arrested meant nothing. Don't list it on employment applications or speak of it."

## Can you identify **Minimizing, Denying and Blaming?**

_____

_____

_____

_____

_____

_____

_____

_____

_____

_____

## Economic Abuse:

- Preventing her from getting or keeping a job.
- Making her ask for money.
- Giving her an allowance.
- Taking her money.
- Not letting her know about or have access to family income.

## POLICE THREAT

Saturday was a sunshine, blue sky day. Wade and I got a phone call. Janelle asked us to take Landen on our day trip because Rashad was acting up. The night before, Janelle went out with the girls then to the 24-hour big box store. She got home at three a.m. Rashad was not impressed and went off asking such things as, "Who were you out f*****g tonight, I hope his d**k was good." And it started from there and continued until it was time for work.

She was working at an apartment complex as a rental agent. It was a temporary position, but one she was doing well. The office staff seemed to like her and possibly wanted to keep her on after the assignment was complete.

Janelle called me for help. Rashad was at the apartment complex threatening her, yelling for her to come outside the office, and making a spectacle of himself. She was afraid to go outside for fear he would attack her. The office manager wanted to call the police, but Janelle persuaded them not to, for fear that his after work violence would be worse. The office could not let it continue. When the office stated they were going to call the police, he left.

Janelle asked me to go to the bank and withdraw all her money before Rashad does it, as he had done in the past. I took her to the bank to handle her business. Janelle goes back to work, and Rashad brings Landen with him to her job and clowns again. He clowns so much; the office management calls the police to have him removed from the property.

He leaves saying he is going to Alabama with Landen and she will never see him again. Janelle is upset. She wants to report her car stolen, it's the car he is driving. The police say after 24 hours Janelle can report it stolen. She cannot file kidnapping charges because he could be taking Landen on vacation.

Janelle and Rashad begin to text each other, it comes out he wants half of the money taken out of the bank. He says if he gets half, then he will let her see Landen.

I couldn't believe he is trying to ransom his son for $650, I couldn't believe it.

Janelle went to the apartment to get her computer, on her way out, they ran into each other and Landen comes to her. A friend sits for Landen until Wade, and I get back in town later that evening. Janelle and Landen bed down at my house for the night.

## Can you identify acts of **Economic Abuse?**

_____

_____

_____

_____

_____

_____

## Using Children:

- Making her feel guilty about the children.
- Using the children to relay messages.
- Using visitation to harass her.
- Threatening to take the children away.

### INDEPENDENCE vs. SUPPORT

During the separation and before the divorce there was little contact between Janelle and Rashad. Janelle was living at home and Wade, and I was helping her as much as possible. She was dealing with the marriage coming to a legal end. She stayed with us as long as she needed. Janelle wanted to contribute financially to the household. She decided to start helping with groceries.

She went searching for help and found herself at the Department of Human Services. They could help her with food stamps and insurance for Landen. Janelle wanted to be as self-sufficient as she could. Things were moving up.

The state of Tennessee sent Rashad a letter saying he was responsible for child support. Rashad contacted Janelle to ask why she put him on child support? She said, "I didn't, I requested food stamps." Rashad told her, "If I wasn't on child support, I could help you more and take me off of it." He tried to make her feel guilty for requesting food stamps since it put him in the child support register.

The state was requesting child support from Rashad. Janelle asked for food stamps, two different things. Rashad would have to contact the State of Tennessee for further consideration.

Janelle and Landen were ready to move out on their own. The cost of an apartment and the bills that come with it were more than expected. Janelle needed some help. The food stamps and insurance were a big help. Wade and I contributed where we could. Rashad wasn't helping with Landen. He had another family to take care of.

At this time, Janelle and Landen have received no regular payments.

## Can you identify the **Use of Children?**

_____

_____

_____

_____

_____

_____

_____

_____

_____

_____

_____

_____

## Coercion and Threats:

- Making and/or carrying out threats to do something to hurt her.
- Threatening to leave her, commit suicide, or report her to welfare.
- Making her drop charges.
- Making her do illegal things.

## EVICTION

Rashad had a problem with Janelle's housekeeping. It became a point of contention in their marriage. Whenever an argument started, it seemed to always be two issues. The original issue and housekeeping. He always complained about it, stating he didn't live that way when he lived alone. When they lived together, the housekeeping was still her downfall. Though it did not seem to bother him living in her campus apartment, while in Alabama.

The day Janelle was dragged the final time from the apartment by Rashad, she left her furniture there. She didn't have money for a moving van, workers, or a storage unit. Jannelle didn't have to pay out any money if she left the furniture there. She felt if he destroyed the furniture she would have to work it out, but in the meantime, she would keep her fingers crossed.

They were in Chattanooga, divorcing and living apart. One day she received a text message from him stating if she wanted her furniture she had 24 hours to get it before the apartment complex padlocked the door for eviction. Janelle tried to work it out. She called friends to get money for a moving truck and to help her move furniture. She called her parents again and explained the situation. Wade had used a same day furniture moving company previously. They had availability for that day. The move was on.

When Janelle and Trisha, Janelle's friend, first investigated the apartment, it looked like a cyclone had been through it. Janelle felt it was unfair all the times Rashad complained of her housekeeping and he was no better. He knew her housekeeping skills from Alabama, and now he is not showing any better. His housekeeping was like Janelle's.

He came to Chattanooga with only a suitcase. Janelle furnished the apartment with the furniture she inherited from her grandparents. He thought she would lose the furniture, having only 24 hours to remove it. Losing the furniture would have threatened the memory of Janelle's grandparents.

Can you identify any **Coercion and Threats?**

_____

_____

_____

_____

_____

_____

_____

_____

_____

## Male Privilege:

- Treating her like a servant.
- Making all the big decisions.
- Acting as the "master of the castle"
- Being the one to define men's and women's roles.

### DIVORCE COURT

Janelle wanted to talk to her dad and me one day. She told us she wanted a divorce but didn't know how to go about the process. Her dad found her a good divorce attorney that came highly recommended for protecting her client's assets. There was Landen to consider.

Janelle didn't want her child, Landen, to become a pawn in the adult issues. Attorney Jones made sure Landen remained with his mother, and no further problem existed.

Before the court date, Janelle was trying to figure out her next step. Janelle and Rashad were living in two separate locations. She was still very emotional and hurting. She was trying to dismiss the thought of him.

As mentioned, Rashad had another child, Mark, in Alabama. He was being cared for by his mother. Janelle previously was sending financial gifts to him. She stopped sending gifts and let Rashad take care of his son since they were divorcing. Rashad hadn't been responsible for Mark except for an occasional phone call, according to Janelle.

Janelle and Landen were at my house. One day a car came to my house, and it was Rashad. He wanted to take Landen for the day. Janelle asked if he had a car seat. His reply was "no." Her reply was "no until you get a car seat." He fussed, cussed, got back into the car, and sped off. Janelle heard it through the grapevine that he was seeing someone, she was pregnant. She was in the car the day he came to get

Landen, and she was staying at the apartment with him.

It's the hearing date, everyone shows up: Janelle, her attorney, Wade and me, Rashad, and his pregnant girlfriend. Rashad does divorce research and acts as his own attorney. The court finds most items in favor of Janelle. Rashad received supervised visitation. He thought he could outsmart the judge and the attorney.

## Can you identify the actions of **Male Privilege?**

_____

_____

_____

_____

_____

_____

_____

_____

_____

_____

_____

_____

# Notes from Mom

Yesterday and last night was a rough one. I realize I must stop alienating Janelle, but it's hard. I'm taking my feelings out on her, and this is the time I need to be supportive. It is hard to be supportive when I feel she made a huge mistake.

I applaud her for trying to keep her family together but with him, yuck. Do I want them to divorce? I don't know. This way, she knows what she is dealing with, Rashad. With someone else, the learning curve starts all over again. What if she attracts the same type of person or worse? I don't know.

All I know is, she needs her parents to be in her corner, mistakes or no mistakes. Life is too short to be unhappy, get the divorce.

# Master Manipulators - What Abusers Say?

Master manipulators have many tricks to coerce their victims into doing what they want, whether it is reconciling, having sex or sitting at home with no one to talk to. They will use whatever means necessary to get or keep the victim under their control. Abusers may use the following statements to get victims to stay or come back into their lives:

- I'll kill myself if you leave.
- I love you, and it will never happen again.
- No one will ever want you.
- If you leave me, I'll kill your family.
- No one is going to believe you.
- I'll enter a drug treatment program.
- Your love could change me.
- I encouraged her family to talk to her about coming back to me.
- We could go to church together.
- You will never be rid of me.
- You're wrong, and that's all there is to it.
- I don't need you, you need me.
- I make the decisions around here.
- You wouldn't want anything to happen to them children.
- If you ever decided to leave me, no one will ever find you.
- I have already talked to our pastor, and he's on my side.
- I must have sex, and it's your duty to give it to me.
- You can't manage money, so I must keep you out of the accounts.

- The Bible says you must have sex with me, so do it.
- This abuse is a family matter, no one needs to know about it.
- Why do you make me hurt you?
- God will get you if you don't come back to me.

**What else could Abusers say?**

_____

_____

_____

_____

_____

_____

_____

_____

Jeremiah 29:11

"For surely I know the plans for your
welfare and not for harm, to give you a future
with hope."

# **<u>Down & Dirty Notes</u>**

# Chapter 4

# Getting Ready

*"Use the dirt life throws at you to plant the seeds of your success."*
**Matshona Dhliwayo**

# Start Now and Prepare

Be prepared in case something happens. Memorize or key essential numbers into your phone, both mobile, and land-line. Update your contact list. If you have an address book, take time to update it as well. Take a few minutes to decide what numbers and information you need and key/write them **NOW**. Don't wait. In an emergency, your phone can be your life-line. Download an app and look up websites to aid in your emergency information.

### 911  Notify Police

Call, in case of an emergency or if you witness someone needing help. When calling, be sure to **give your location, your phone number, and details** of why you're calling. Some phones either don't have or have the "high accuracy" location finder turned off. The location finder uses GPS, Wi-Fi, Bluetooth, your number and carrier's network to find you.

### 211  Worldwide United Way - www.unitedway.org

**211.org** to find local services and get help today. For Canada, please visit uww.211.ca.

All calls are free, private and confidential. The professional answering your call will be live and highly trained. They are an essential resource to help in a personal crisis. The service helps people in North America and worldwide find resources in their area 24 hours a day, 7 days a week.

### 1+800-799-7233 National Domestic Violence Hotline

The hotline is a 24-hour confidential service that offers a variety of life-saving services. The hotline can be reached by phone or online.

**(fill in your information)**
**"ICE" (In Case Of Emergency)** _____

It should be your main emergency contact: a parent, close friend, or neighbor. The person you want to be notified in case something happens to you. Many emergency personnel knows to look for this number in your phone.

**Home landline**, if there is one. _____

Emergency personnel may try this number as an alternative number to the "ICE" number. If someone finds your phone, he or she can call this number to let you know your phone is intact.

**Highway Patrol** _____

Call the state highway patrol for assistance, if stranded on the side of the road.

**Motor Club** _____

Your motor club can give you roadside assistance, help with flat tires, and if keys are locked in the car.

**Local Domestic Violence Shelter** _____

Consider your needs for the holidays and pets.

**A friend, co-worker, or family member** _____

This is someone you can call in a crisis that will come to your aid or act as a witness. Have a "Safe" word or phrase you can use. Keep it short and not difficult.

**Download a safety app.**

There are several apps for women's or men's safety. Some are free or cost a fee using your Android or iPhone. The apps can do different things such as:

1. Call police if a phone call is disconnected.
2. Locate taxi, or an on-demand private driver, Uber, Lyft, near you.
3. Send messages to emergency contacts.
4. Select panic buttons.
5. Send emails and messages on Facebook.
6. And more

**DomesticShelters.org** _____

Will search more than 3,000 Domestic Violence programs to help find those offering pet shelter.

**Clergy** _____
**Use the space below to list others**

_____

_____

_____

_____

_____

_____

_____

# An Example of Hometown Services

## Chattanooga, Tennessee

The Partnership for Families, Children and Adults has 5 centers of integrated services; Victim Support, Elder Support, Mission Driven Enterprises, Deaf, and Stability services. Under the Victim Support services currently is a Domestic Violence 101 class. The participants of the class are led by an instructor and the open forum is inviting. Participants share history and talk through issues of concern. Literature is handed out and discussed. An interpreter is available, if needed.

The instructor encourages participation but understands not everyone is ready and willing to discuss his or her own situation. "The Partnership assists survivors with personal safety planning, emotional support, legal rights, safe housing and the ability to believe in and rely on themselves." All services are free and LGBTQ friendly.

The Chattanooga Hamilton County Family Justice Center stated they offer free services to those experiencing Domestic Violence, elder abuse, or human trafficking.

Both organizations working together aid Domestic Violence victims to give the best possible care. Multiple locations are available, and their office hours may vary. **The Crisis Hotline is available 24/7. It can be reached in the Chattanooga area at 423-755-2700.**

**The National Domestic Violence Hotline number is 1+800-799-7233.**

## What Services are Available in your Area or Community?

_____

_____

_____

_____

_____

_____

_____

_____

_____

_____

_____

_____

_____

_____

We are here to listen...not work miracles.

We are here to help a woman discover what she is feeling...not to make the feelings go away.

We are here to help a woman identify her options...not to decide for her what she should do.

We are here to discuss steps with a woman...not to take steps for her.

We are here to help a woman discover her own strength...not to rescue her and leave her still vulnerable.

We are here to help a woman discover she can help herself...not to take responsibility for her.

We are here to help a woman learn to choose...not to keep her from making difficult choices.

We are here to provide support for change.

-*Anonymous*

Produced and distributed by the National Center on Domestic and Sexual Violence
(512)407-9020 • www.ncdsv.org

## Exit Preparedness

Preparing to leave your home is and isn't an easy decision. The decision is easier if your situation is such that the safety of you and your children are at risk. High anxiety can set in, when not prepared for your exit. Planning can ease some anxiety of exiting now or later. It would be beneficial to have items as money, and always a charged cell phone with the connector cord or charger, important phone numbers in your contact list, medicine, clothing, relevant information and other items you deem necessary in a safe, secure place outside the home.

Have an escape plan and practice it.

- Start now and begin to prepare by making copies and securing the following documents:
- Birth certificates, Social Security cards, passports or immigration papers for you and your children
- Orders of Protection
- Medical insurance cards for you and your children
- Financial records, stock, mutual fund records, and recent bank statements
- Title or deed statements, rental agreements
- Your credit reports
- Your car paperwork, title, or lease
- Retirement plan paperwork
- Tax returns for the past two years
- A written copy of important phone numbers, and addresses in case you can't get to your phone

Many of the above documents can be replaced by phone, online, by mail or the replacement needs to be requested in person.

- Start with your driver's license or state identification card.

- Your vehicle registration will need the license plate number and the vehicle identification number, (found in the driver's front window, near the hood.)

- Your passport requires identification and a photo to be re-placed.

Keep access to these accounts to retrieve them at your discretion. If others have access to your email account, you may start a new account that only you have the password to an email a copy of the documents to yourself. Most cities have public computers in libraries and cafés.

Banks have safe deposit boxes you can use for valuable assets. You can keep valuable jewelry in the box or with you. Take pictures of home assets, and anything you think is worth money.

While preparing the necessary paperwork to leave the residence, remember your significant other can still be in the immediate area, and caution needs to be taken. Continue to try to defuse confrontational situations. Walking away may de-escalate the situation. A friend, family member, or neighbor may help also. They can run interference, be an audience, accompany another person, if needed, or be on standby. By becoming part of the plan, a friend can give some relief, be a back-up for the number one back-up, give a sense of friendship and, most of all, support.

If the household pet needs to travel with you, gather their items also such as tags, medical records, leashes, food, and medicine.

Practice your exit!!!!!

Practice, Practice, Practice!

**Use the space below to make your Get Ready List:**

_____

_____

_____

_____

_____

_____

_____

_____

_____

_____

_____

_____

_____

_____

_____

# 7 Stages of Grief

The 7 Stages of Grief serves as a guide of transition from one stage to the next. It is used when one relationship ends, whether it is a marriage, death, or a loss of some kind. The stages are interchangeable, overlapping, or repeated. There is no real order to the stages people go through. We are all unique individuals and the grieving process is unique with each of us.

Outsiders may feel it's time to be over a loss. The stages take time, months, years, sometimes many years. Only you can determine when it is time to move to the next step.

Find an outlet along the way. Support groups or journaling may help you to see beyond yesterday. You are your own "Cinderella or Prince Charming."

The ultimate goal is to get to the 7th stage of acceptance. At that time life looks a little brighter and you can move forward with the New You.

**The stages are:**
1.  **Shock and Denial -** Disbelief is universal. To avoid pain, you may deny the reality of the loss. Shock provides an emotional shield from being overwhelmed.
2.  **Pain and Guilt -** Pain replaces the shock and is a necessary procedure to experience. Drowning this experience with alcohol or drugs is not recommended. Guilt can bring feelings of regret. Regretting things, you did or didn't do to make the relationship work can make life seem confused and scary.
3.  **Anger and Bargaining -**Transferring emotion and frustration can lead to extreme violence. Relationship damage may be the result of the transferring of rage to others. You may

want to ask, "Why me?" and try using it as a bargaining chip to reduce hopelessness. "I'll go to church every Sunday if you bring him back."

4. **Depression, Reflection, Loneliness-** The enormity of losing the relationship sets in. Isolation, sadness, and the feeling of emptiness can overwhelm you. The reflection of the past becomes a focal point.

5. **The Upward Turn -** The depression begins to lessen, and life starts to become calmer. Your physical symptoms begin to decrease.

6. **Reconstruction and Working Through -** Starting to seek realistic solutions to life's problems begin. You will become more functional. Thoughts of being without your loved one begins.

7. **Acceptance and Hope -** Reality sets in and you will begin to move forward. Your future looks brighter. You will start to plan, anticipate and experience joy.

*2 Timothy 4:17*

*But the Lord stood by me and gave me strength, so that through me the message might be fully proclaimed, and all the Gentiles might hear it. So I was rescued from the lion's mouth.*

# **<u>Down & Dirty Notes</u>**

# Chapter 5

# Janelle's Reflections

*"Don't be afraid of being alone; remember, when the sun rises, it rises with nobody at its side."*
**Matshona Dhliwayo**

# Janelle on the 7 Stages of Grief

I am my daughter's biggest fan. I wanted to find out how she moved from marriage, domestic violence and starting over to the happy person she is today. I am very thankful she was able to find friends in her life that was able to support her.

**MOM -** After the marriage ended, did you go through the 7 stages of grief?

**JANELLE** - I did not go through all the stages. I'll take them one at a time.

**1. Shock:** I think I was angrier. Rashad got married 17 days after the divorce to his pregnant girlfriend. I was hurt because this was clearly adultery.

**2. Denial:** I didn't experience denial. I knew we were ending because he didn't follow through with the counseling classes needed for marriage success.

**3. Bargaining:** There was no deal. I did everything I knew to do to make my marriage work. He committed adultery, I did not want him back.

**4. Anger:** There was no real anger of the marriage ending, just issues.

**5. Depression:** Yes, when I was going through it, I did not recognize it was depression. Looking back on it, yes, I was depressed. I joined a new church, found renewed faith, and the positivity of new friends brought me out of the depression. The pastor publicly acknowledged the beauty and essence of his wife. That sparked a light within me, and it encouraged me to have a personal relationship with God.

**6. Guilt:** No, I had no guilt. I tried.

**7. Acceptance:** During our separation before the divorce, Rashad was still making promises he wasn't going to keep. I had to do what's right for my son and myself. Rashad was a master manipulator.

**MOM** -What are your takeaways, both positive and negative, of your marriage?

**JANELLE** - I enjoyed being married and still believe in the institution.

**MOM** - Was there any violence or red flags, when you were dating?

**JANELLE** - Yes, anger was a red flag. I ignored this during dating. We had different upbringings and backgrounds. Our thought processes were also different.

**MOM** - Was there anything your parents could have done differently, in preparing you for life?

**JANELLE** - I never saw any unhealthy marriages. I didn't know my arguments were unhealthy until I shared some things with a friend.

**MOM** - What was the final straw?

**JANELLE** - The final straw was when he dragged me from the back to the front of the apartment, yelling, "Get the 'F' out." Divorce was never an option until he drug me. Physical abuse was the last straw. The other violence was probably evenly distributed.

# Messages from Janelle Shared
# Over the Internet

2015

**JANELLE:**

I couldn't let this day end without this brief testimony!! It was July 5, 2015 that I took the GREATEST step in my Christian walk. I experienced water baptism. I wasn't at my home church. I didn't tell my family. Instead, I followed the instruction of the Holy Spirit and went to the Alabaster Campus of the Church of the Highlands in Birmingham and got baptized. And since that day, I swear God has opened more doors than ever before. That day I decided to live and to live in purpose. Thus, Happy Birthday to me! I chose to live!!

2016

**JANELLE:**

Did you know that October is NOT ONLY Breast Cancer Awareness Month, but is ALSO Domestic Violence Awareness Month…? Probably not, but I want you all to know that Domestic Violence is NOT just a black eye, busted lip, or physical abuse! Domestic Violence is also mental abuse, emotional abuse, and any other type of behavior used to maintain power and control over an intimate partner. It's not just male to female, females can be abusers too! Just open your eyes and know that your friend, sister, brother, mother, cousin, ANYONE can be crying out to you for help! God did not create us to live in fear, we have POWER in HIM, and there is POWER to get out of a bad situation. When my eyes were opened, I was covered by the Holy Spirit and was able to get OUT! It was ONLY the blood of Jesus that protected me in bad situations. It was me LEANING on The Word that brought me through the hurt and pain! And it is GOD'S GRACE that is mending a broken heart. Don't get me wrong, BREAST CANCER hits home really tough, my Grandma Enelle, Aunt Delores, and Cousin DeVon CONTINUE to rest in paradise. I miss you all dearly, yet I KNOW that you are rejoicing with the KING!!! Have a good day and Happy Domestic Violence Awareness Month!!!

2016

**JANELLE:**

I'm a firm believer that God puts people in your life for reasons, seasons, blessings, and lessons. And my Lord, if He doesn't make it clear when that time comes to an end, and you are free to remove yourself from the situation!! My God!! #Confirmation #Growth

2017

**JANELLE:**

In 2008, I married the man I assumed to be the love of my life. In 2009 I went to jail for domestic assault because I was defending myself. In 2010 my glasses were ripped off my face and broken, my luggage was thrown in the dumpster, and my tires were flattened when I was trying to leave. In 2011 he drugged me from the back bedroom of our home telling me to get the "bleep" out. April 10, 2012, at 8:36 a.m., we were divorced… April 2017 I heard him "apologize for all the hell he put me through from 2008 to now". Domestic Violence is real yall!!! Every story is different, but it's never nullified!!! #Survived #DomesticViolence #DVAM #ForgivenessIsFreeing #BeautyForAshes.

2017

**JANELLE:**

As a divorced mom, I never want anyone to experience the hurt I endured!!! Not necessarily because of him, but because of my lack of submission, my lack of conversation, I not knowing how to be a wife, my not caring about learning the duties of a wife, allowing my emotions to get the best of me, not trusting nor caring to trust Him, and not having a SOLID relationship with Christ, just to name a few…. thus I endured the HELL of a Godless marriage. It didn't matter that we were in ministry, it mattered that WE didn't have a solid relationship with Christ as a couple. Married couples going through a rough patch have been on the lips of my prayers for a while now…. And if you need or want some specific prayer slide through my DM… I want that Lord that reigns over my life to be the same Lord that reigns over your marriage!!!! Love Y'all!!!!

# Letter to Janelle

Dear Janelle,

I wanted to write this letter to explain and give more detail to some of the pages in this book. I wrote about the things I saw, heard, and felt. You lived the experiences and may have an entirely different viewpoint. As we are individuals and our lives mingle, you will have your own story to tell.

I'm very old school, meaning I have traditional values. Wanting you to finish college before beginning your family, was more than a notion. I've seen how starting a family can derail a career, earning financial freedom, and travel. This may not seem as necessary, but it divides your concentration. The saying, "you cannot serve two masters" comes to mind. Your decision was made when you got pregnant. This is the twenty-first century, and no one gets pregnant unless they are willing to accept the consequences, rape is an exception.

I accepted your pregnancy, I couldn't love Landen more. Rashad appeared sincere to you when you and he stood in God's eyes for marriage. After you two said "I do" the atmosphere of your relationship changed. It seemed you thought of him as an extension of you, friend, or neighbor. Some of what was yours was his, and he thought what yours was, was his also, including what your parents had, to an extent.

You were learning to make your own money and becoming self-reliant. Rashad, I learned was used to making his way on the backs of others. I didn't understand coming to a new city with no money or job prospects. He talked a good game, and we let him stay because of you.

Stress was beginning. Rashad began to ask me, and Wade questions such as "how do you make her listen, and how do you make her do other things?" The honeymoon phase was ending, and the tension phase was beginning. The yelling started. This drove me crazy and made me scared for you and Landen. I yelled at you and Gary, as kids," clean your room, pick up your clothes" but you never heard me and your father yell at each other.

I thought we showed you, true love. How did it get reversed where you showed Rashad love for a king, and he showed you servant love? In my eyes, he did not treat you like a queen, and you let him. I didn't understand. I wanted to shake some sense into you and shake the puddin' out of him.

When the abuse started, I tried to let you figure it out, but it was ongoing. I felt helpless. I didn't know where to turn. I didn't want to bother Gary away in school. I wanted him to concentrate on his studies. No one I talked to had any suggestions but to listen. I regularly spoke to Wade and coworkers. Wade tried to stay calm. His fear was going to jail because of hurting Rashad. The chain reaction of me not being able to maintain a household and possibly becoming homeless restrained Wade's actions. I wanted to buy a gun and use it. I was afraid of not going to heaven because of taking a life. My co-workers became tired of hearing the same conversation. Finally, I decided to contact my company Employee Assistance Program (EAP) and speak to a counselor.

The counseling sessions didn't go well. The counselor seemed to be more interested in the audacity of the stories. She was absorbing what you went through as described in the power and control wheel examples and the other issues of abuse. I needed help in finding a way to destress and help you. Eventually, I stopped going. Now I know I should have requested another counselor and another, and another until I was able to find the one to help me get the answers I needed.

I pray to never again let someone have that amount or type of power over me and you too. I gave up with the counselor leaving me to my own devices, which was to stand back and watch. I was there when you came to me but, I didn't step in to prevent the abuse. For this, I am genuinely sorry. Not stepping in may have given Rashad the idea it was ok to treat you less than your worth.

With many tears and much prayer, you were able to come through this season in your life. It was only when you began to heal, I started to improve. I understand the healing process may take a while, possibly many years. After 10 years, I still remember the events and talking about them make me cry. I have post-traumatic stress disorder (PTSD), a self-diagnosis, you may also.

Janelle, know there is help out there, you have to seek it and keep searching until you find answers and are satisfied. I will always be here for you and will do my best for you and Landen. I love you both.

You met a man, fell in love, married him, and had a child. The relationship didn't turn out the way you thought it would. By saying "I DO," I think you both thought some things about each other would change. It didn't, and the trauma started. Change can only happen if you want it and try wholeheartedly to do it. You cannot change another person if they are resistant to change.

You are a queen. Don't let anyone treat you any less. I will always love you,

Mom

## Notes from Mom

My beautiful, God-fearing, daughter Janelle was a

**Lover,**

**Wife,**

**Victim,**

And is now a

**Mother,**

and a

**Survivor.**

# <u>Down & Dirty Notes</u>

_____

_____

_____

_____

_____

_____

_____

_____

_____

_____

_____

_____

_____

_____

_____

# **Down & Dirty Notes**

_____

_____

_____

_____

_____

_____

_____

_____

_____

_____

_____

_____

_____

_____

# Resources

## Chapter 1

- *New Revised Standard Version Bible*. Grand Rapids: Zondervan, 1989. Print.

- Sennott, Laurie Jean. "Find & Share Quotes with Friends." n.d. *https://www.good-reads.com/quotes/search?utf8=%E2%9C%93&q=laurie+jean+sennott&commit=Search*. Document. 15 May 2018.

- "Historically Black Colleges and Universities: 1976 to 1994." *National Center for Education Statistics* July 1996: table 8, pp. 30. Document. 25 July 2018.

- Grohol, John M., Psy.D. "6 Tips to Improve Your Self-Esteem." n.d. *https://psychcentral.com/blog/6-tips-to-improve-your-self-esteem/*. Document. 13 May 2018.

- Lyon, Kim. "Recognizing Low Self-Esteem." 15 December 2015. *http://explorable.com/e/recognizing-low-self-esteem?gid=21367*. Document. 25 July 2018.

- Bellenonds, Colleen de. "Here's How Your Organs Move to Make Room for Baby During Each Week of Your Pregnancy." October 2016. *https://www.whattoexpect.com/wom/pregnancy/this-is-how-your-organs-move-to-make-room-for-baby-every-week-of-pregnancy#4*. Document. 13 May 2018.

- "Domestic Violence." n.d. *https://everytownresearch.org/issue/domestic-violence/*. Document. 25 July 2018.

- Kerry, Shaw. "12 Facts That Show How Guns Make Domestic Violence Even Deadlier." 22 08 2016. *https://The-trace.org/2016/08/domestic-violence-gun-facts.* Document. 19 July 2018.

- "What Is Domestic Violence." n.d. *https://www.domesticviolenceroundtable.org/whatisdv.* Document. 13 May 2018.

- Samsel, Michael. "Gaslighting." 2008-2018. *https://www.abuseandrelationships.org/Content/The_Con/gaslighting.html.* Document. 25 July 2018.

- Vann, M. Susan Ph.D. "The Impact of Domestic Violence in the Workplace." Seventh Annual DOE contractor EAP Training. 2018. Document.

- *New Revises Standard Version Bible.* Grand Rapids: Zondervan, 1989. Print.

## Chapter 2

- Dhliwayo, Matshona. "Find & Share Quotes with Friends." n.d. *https://www.goodreads.com/quotes/search?utf8=%E2%9C%93&q=use+the+dirt+life+throws&commit=Search.* Document. 15 May 2018.

- Legge, Jessica. "Domestic violence: On average, they go back seven times." 18 October 2006. *www.timeswv.com/news/local_news/domestic-violence-on-average-they-go-back-seven-times/article_b375ded6-84a8-5a9c-8c85-9405d08789df.html.* Document. 13 May 2018.

- Olsen, Erica. "Strategic Implementation." n.d. *https://onstrategyhq.com/resources/strategic-implementation/.* Document. 13 May 2018.

- Grohol, John M., Psy.D. "Psych Central 6 Tips to Improve

Your Self-Esteem." 25 October 2011. *https://psychcentral.com/blog/6-tips-to-improve-your-self-esteem/*. Document. 20 July 2018.

- Staff, Mayo Clinic. "Self-esteem: Take steps to feel better about yourself." n.d. *https://www.mayoclinic.org/healthy-lifestyle/adult-health/in-depth/self-esteem/art-20045374*. Document. 13 May 2018.

- Thum, Myrko. "What Are Your Personal Strengths and Weaknesses?" 5 March 2013. *www.myrkothum.com/?s=personal+strengths+and+weaknesses*. Document. 20 July 2018.

## Chapter 3

- Moore, Beth. "smart and relentless." 15 July 2016. *http://smartandrelentless.com/20-inspiration-beth-moore-quotes-dirt-is-dirt-and-weve-all-got-it-no-matter-where-we-come-from/*. Document. 8 August 2018.

- Goldsmith, Toby D., MD. "Psych Central The Common Pattern of Domestic Violence." 2016. *https://psychcentral.com/lib/the-common-pattern-of-domestic-violence*. Document. 20 July 2018.

- "Power and Control Wheel." n.d. *www.ncdsv.org*. Document. 20 July 2018.

- "Things Abusers Say and Do to Gain Power Over You." n.d. *verbalabusejournals.com/about-abuse/things-abusers-say-do/*. Document. 20 July 2018.

- *New Revised Standard Version Bible*. Grand Rapids: Zondervan, 1989. Print.

## Chapter 4

- "Goodreads." 18 March 2018. *https://www.goodreads.com/author/quotes/7978664.Matshona_Dhliwayo?page=2.* Document. 12 August 2018.

- "Emergency Phone Number List." n.d. *https://www.nationwide.com/cell-phone-numbers.jsp.* Document. 13 May 2018.

- "National Link Coalition Safety Planning for Pets." n.d. *www.domesticshelters.org/domestic-violence-articles-information/planning-for-pets-safety.* Document. 20 July 2018.

- Coopersmith, Tristan. "How to Survive All Seven Stages of a Brutal Breakup." 21 February 2017. Document. 13 May 2018.

- "Find Quotes." n.d. *https://www.goodreads.com/quotes/search?utf8=%E2%9C%93&q=every+seed+must+rise+through+dirt+to+enjoy+the+sunshine&commit=Search.* Document. 20 July 2018.

- "Domestic Violence Resources." n.d. *Domestic Violence Roundtable.* Document. 13 May 2018.

- Leon, Ross. "How to Avoid Making the Same Mistake Twice." n.d. *Girls Chase Forum.* Document. 13 May 2018.

- "Domestic Violence Roundtable." n.d. *www.domesticviolenceroundtable.org/whatisdv.* Document. 20 July 2018.

- *Partnership for Families Children and Adults.* Chattanooga, 13 May 2018. Document.

- Neason, Matt. "Outcome Goals vs Process Goals." 1 July 2013. *www.sportpsychologytoday.com/sports-psychology-articles/outcome-goals-vs-process-goals/.* Document. 25 July 2018.

- *New Revised Standard Version Bible.* Grand Rapids: Zondervan, 1989. Print.

- "Partnership for Families, children and Adults." (2018). pamphlet.
- Regina. "The Pixel Project's "16 For 16" Campaign." 10 December 2012. *16days.thepixelproject.net/16-safety-ideas-and-tips-for-women-facing-domestic-violence-over-the-holiday-season/*. Document. 13 May 2018.
- "Leaving an abusive relationship, What do I need to include in my safety packing list?" n.d. *https://www.Women-shealth.gov/relationships-and-safety/domestic-violence/leaving-abusive-relation...* Document. 13 May 2018.
- "My House Caught on Fire: How do I Replace Personal Documents after a Fire?" n.d. *http://firedamageprop-ertyaz.com/blog.html/2014/12/31/my-house-caught-on-fire-how-do-i-replace.* Document. 20 July 2018.
- Thum, Myrko. "What Are Your Personal Strengths and Weaknesses?" 5 March 2013. *www.myrkothum.com/?s=personal+strengths+and+weaknesses.* Document. 20 July 2018.
- Wright-Parker, Jennie, RN, MSCC, GC-C. "7 Stages of Grief Through the Process and Back to Life." n.d. *https://www.re-cover-from-grief-.com/7-stages-of-grief.html.* Document. 9 August 2018.

# About the Author

Margaret M. Hodges was born in Mount Vernon, New York. She is married and has two beautiful children and two fantastic grandchildren. She earned a Master's Degree in Business Administration from the University of Phoenix Online, Bachelor's Degree from Bennett College, and an Associates Degree from Wade's College.

After retiring from corporate America, Margaret had time to birth this book. Margaret's mother, Edna, told her "life can make you sometimes feel lower than dirt, you have to find a way to turn it around and rise above it to a sunshine blue-sky day." That's the Down and Dirty and turning it around 180°.